CHARLIE

Book 2

"No Dogs on the Bed"

CAROL LEMON

To order additional copies of this book, contact:
Xlibris
844-714-8691
www.Xlibris.com
Orders@Xlibris.com

ISBN: 978-1-6641-8017-8 (sc)
ISBN: 978-1-6641-8018-5 (hc)
ISBN: 978-1-6641-8016-1 (e)

Print information available on the last page

Rev. date: 06/11/2021

Hi, I'm Charlie. This is the story of my adventure on a road trip from Fairbanks AK to Redmond WA. It can be subtitled, "No dogs on the bed."

Overview of the trip.

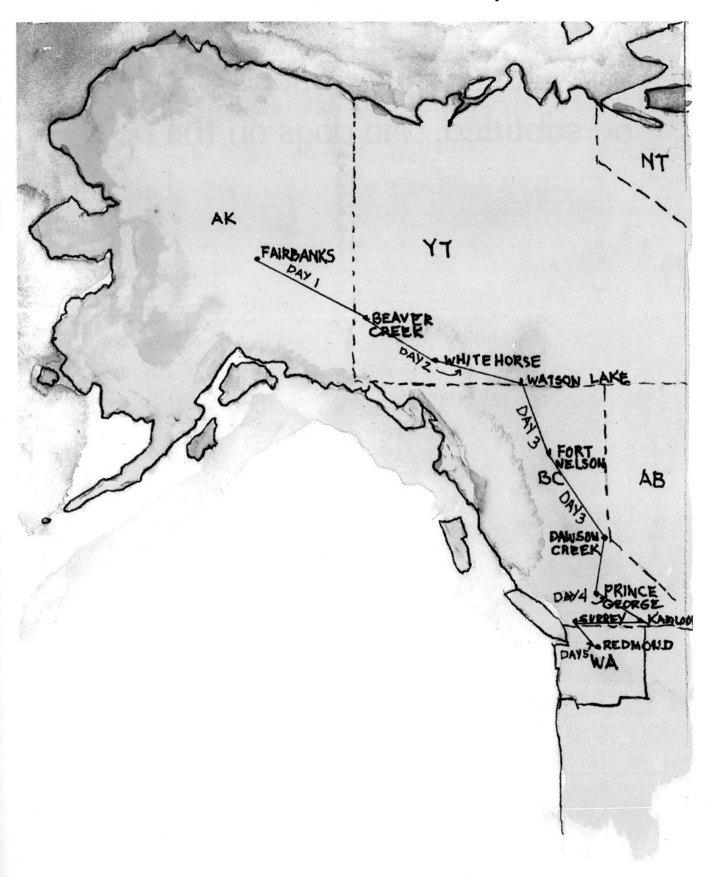

Day One. Mom and I left Fairbanks on Dec 12. Mom and I made the trip in a Honda Civic, but there wasn't room for the crate, so Mom took it apart and put the top in the bottom.

DAY ONE

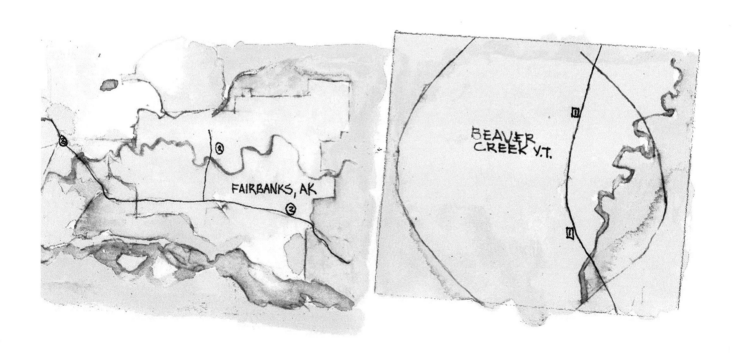

I got good at barking when I needed to potty. Sometimes, though I was surprised by the snow when we stopped for potty breaks.

The first night we stayed at Buckshot Betty's in Beaver Creek, Y.T. I heard the woman say "No dogs on the bed." But I did not care.

The second night we stayed
in White Horse, Y.T.

DAY TWO

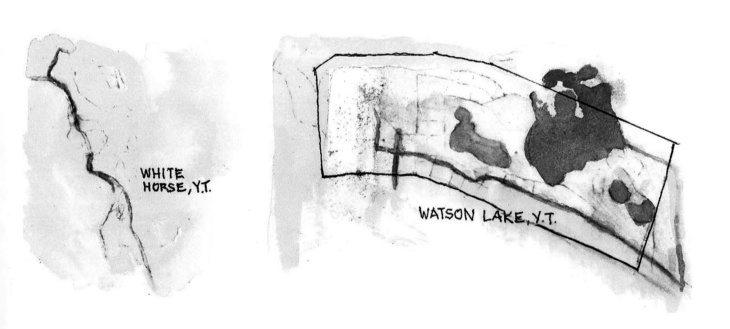

WHITE
HORSE, Y.T.

WATSON LAKE, Y.T.

When we left Fairbanks, AK. I, Charlie, saw two snow leopards in the road in front of the car, but they disappeared into the trees, before we got to them.

Day Two. Mom and I travelled
from White Horse Y.T.

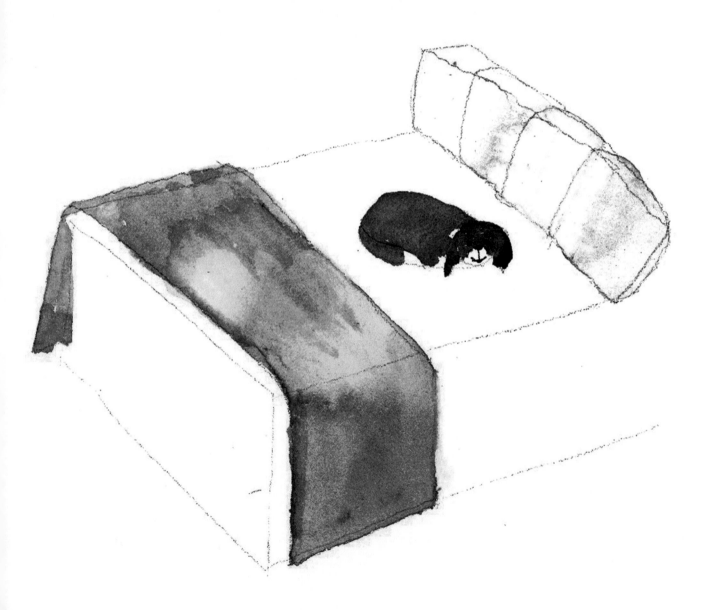

to Watson Lake Y.T.

We went through a forested area in the Nahanni National Park reserve of Canada. We saw a timber buffalo feeding her calf. I was really interested in them, but I had to stay in the car.

Day Three.

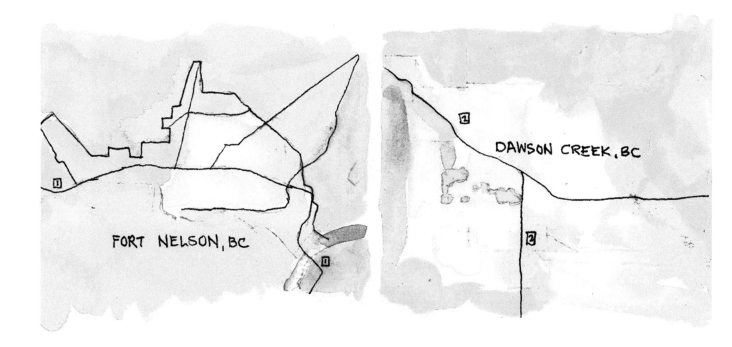

Mom and I travelled from Fort Nelson B.C.

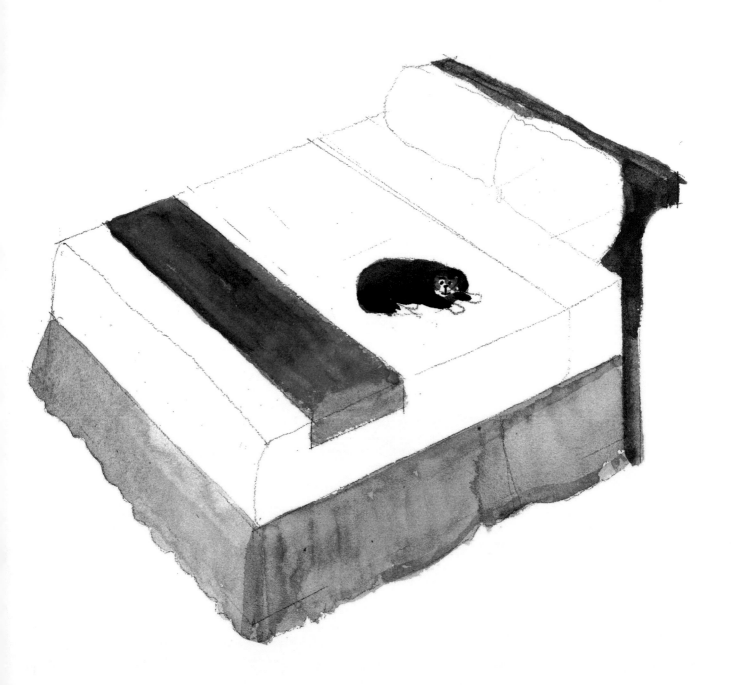

to Dawson Creek B.C.

We went through at forested area in the Nahanni National Park Reserve of Canada. We saw a timber buffalo feeding her calf.

I was interested in them, but Mom would not let me get out of the car.

Day Four.

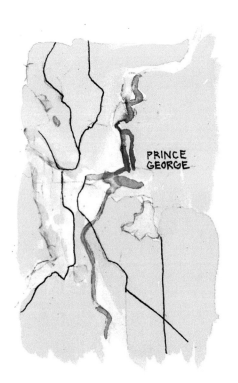

DAY FOUR

PRINCE GEORGE

KAMLOOPS

Mom and I travelled from Prince George B.C.

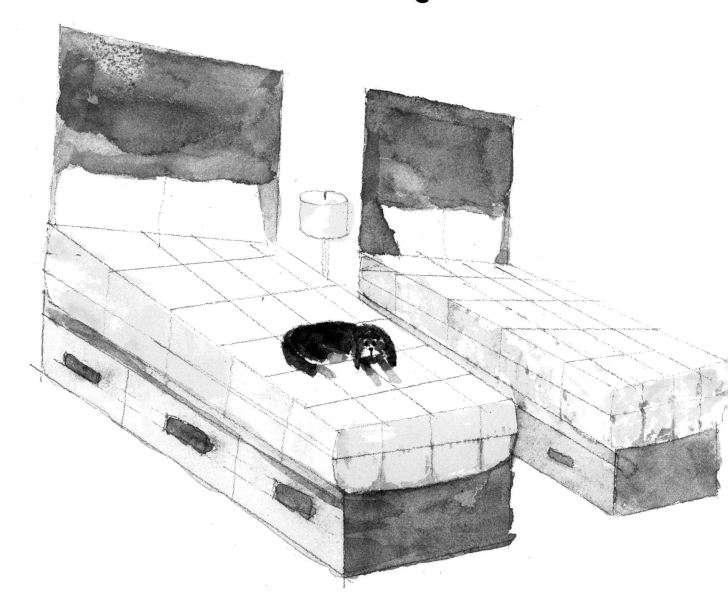

to Kamloops, B.C.

We saw a pair of Mountain goats.

Day Five.

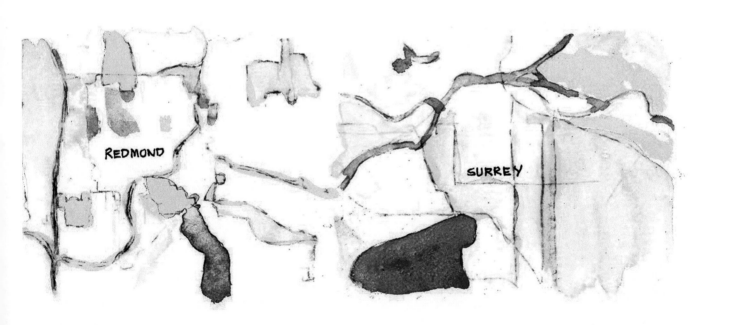

We travelled From Surrey to Redmond.

And so that is the end of the story.

Printed in the United States
by Baker & Taylor Publisher Services